I0786755

Happy Ending Massage:
The Complete Report

Rockit Reports

CONTENTS

Introduction

By all accounts, the practice of massage has been around for millennia in one form or another. Since human beings receive the most pleasure of all from the touch of their genitalia where huge numbers of nerve endings are concentrated, it's not hard to figure out that a good percentage of the countless massages given over the years have concluded with a happy ending.

With so much in traditional massage techniques being rooted in ideas of health and spirituality, it's only natural that many massage practitioners would want their clients to be relieved in every way possible. How beneficial would a massage be if it left you more worked up than you were before you got the massage to begin with? Throw in the modern motivation of making money and you have the perfect recipe for the creation of the vast erotic massage industry that exists today.

Unfortunately, things do not always progress forward in our society. Sometimes they revert or get seriously sidetracked. Today, because of a number of archaic rules and regulations, much of the happy ending industry is somewhat underground. That is, it is hidden in plain sight. Other aspects are more open but still there is little coverage of the industry.

In line with my previous work, I have written this book to share the knowledge I've gained in this field. It's my firm belief that in a free society information should not be restricted and that each of us should be able to make decisions concerning our own lives.

In the following pages you will find a detailed description of the various massage venues that exist around the world starting with massage parlors and providers in the United

States where happy ending massage is for the most part prohibited by law. Most of this is generalized as this is more fitting to a book of this nature.

In this book I report on the ins and outs of happy ending massage venues and providers around the world. I do my best to include all the relevant information. I hope you enjoy.

As should be obvious, my only intention in writing this book and others like it is to share what I've learned in hopes of entertaining the reader.

Neither I nor this book provides any warranty whatsoever, whether express, implied, or statutory. Read at your own risk as a thinking person.

Chinese Massage Parlors

When one thinks of an Asian massage parlor that offers happy endings, their mind most likely conjures up images of Chinese massage parlors, even if they don't know it. Undoubtedly the most common type of massage shop in the United States, Chinese massage parlors exist in every major city and a huge number of suburban and even rural areas.

Massage has been around in China for thousands of years. The *Huangdi Nei-jing*, which is considered the foundation of traditional Chinese medicine, was created sometime between 475 - 220 BC. It contains no less than 30 references to massage. The practice of massage has continued on ever since then in China, even through all of the country's tumultuous history. With the seemingly endless opportunity to make money doing rub downs that exists in the United States, the ancient practice of Chinese massage has been updated, imported and applied widely; a lot like General Tso's Chicken.

When I say Chinese massage parlor I am talking about a particular kind of place. I am not describing every massage parlor with a Chinese name or Chinese people on staff. Obviously there are massage parlors with Chinese names, staff or owners that do not offer anything other than regular old body rubs. On the other hand there are some Chinese owned and staffed places that offer more than just mainstream massages to customers. Those places which have come to be known as "Chinese massage parlors" in circles with an interest in Asian massage parlors are the places I am now describing.

Chinese massage parlors can be found all over the United States. They often provide body massages along with additional erotic services.

Usually single male customers who visit a Chinese

massage parlor will get a poor to decent massage followed by a hand job hand ending finish. On some occasions, especially in "fly by night" setups in residential buildings that come and go from one day to the next, customers may be offered oral sex or even full service.

There are various hints and signs that can help customers figure out whether or not a Chinese massage parlor offers sexual services. If it is open into the late night or early morning or advertises on websites with adult or personal classified ad sections there's a good chance there are extras on offer.

Where extras are on offer at a Chinese massage parlor it's accepted as a normal part of the massage. The logic is that such activity is necessary for "full release" on the part of the male clientele. At least that's the theory. In some cases the simple fact is that masseuses massage particular body parts so that they can make more money in the form of tips than their often meager standard salaries provide otherwise.

Chinese massage parlors often operate in a sort of gray area and service follows as such. These aren't usually straight forward brothels where guys just walk in and get wanked off. Instead they are places where massages are concluded with offers for further work on the parts between the thighs.

This is by design and intended both for the safety of the staff and venues and as a part of creating an overall relaxing atmosphere. After all relaxation is the entire point of massage.

If extras are on offer masseuses will normally make it known. They don't typically wait for customers to make a move. Any guy who shows up at a massage parlor being aggressive and pushing for more than a massage would be asking for trouble. In fact such behavior would probably be illegal and grounds for a masseuse to end a session or even call in law enforcement.

Frequent visitors to happy ending massage parlors in the

United States don't normally ask for any extra services. They simply lay back and receive them as they come. Some masseuses who do offer extra services may even turn down a guy who asks for them directly since they could fear that the customer is in fact a member of some law enforcement agency trying to cause a problem. The law is often among the biggest fears of sex workers in the United States and many other parts of the world for reasons that should be obvious.

Nowadays the internet offers a wide range of information that was not available to massage parlor aficionados even a few years ago. While some guys will still "take one for the team" and visit a massage parlor not covered online to see if they can get a happy ending, the vast majority of customers today research massage parlors in advance in order to find a place to their liking. That has become slightly more difficult with recent laws that have restricted sex related speech on the internet but things are still discussed online rather openly often on websites hosted in countries with speech protections still intact.

When a guy looking for a happy ending enters a massage parlor for the first time they typically ask for a one hour massage. That's true even when a 30 minute massage is available for less money. That is because as a first time visitor they are more likely to get extras with a one hour massage than they are with twenty or thirty minute sessions. Guys who opt for a short session may be branded as a "cheap charlie" off the bat and receive nothing more than a mediocre rub down.

Unlike staff at some Korean massage parlors the women who work at Chinese massage parlors in the United States almost never wear any kind of sexy lingerie. While some of the higher end and better established places may have Chinese women in their twenties in somewhat sexy uniforms on staff the vast majority of Chinese massage parlors have middle aged or even older women working. Of course looks are no indication of skill and some of the oldest women are the most renown for their abilities.

The staff at most Chinese massage parlors will ask unfamiliar customers if they have visited before. Some sources say that guys who want extra service must answer yes to this question no matter what the truth actually is. I don't believe that is true. Guys who say things like "no, but I go to another place" or "no, but my friend told me to come here" seem just as likely to get extra services. Even those who truthfully say "no" and leave it at that are often offered extras.

The usual rate at Chinese massage parlors is 40 to 50 US dollars for an hour massage. Some places may ask for as much as 80 or even 100. There are also some cheaper places around but they are becoming rarer with each passing day. Payment is typically rendered after a massage is given though some places may ask for payment up front if they feel there is a risk of being shorted.

The most high end Chinese massage parlors offer table showers. These involve the customer laying down on a padded table in a wash room and being cleaned from head to toe. Some middle of the road places will allow customers to shower themselves in a private stand up shower before or after the massage. Most places will offer no kind of showering whatsoever.

At the start of massage sessions customers are led to a room and told to take off their clothes. Some rooms are plain but normal with walls that go up to the ceiling and locking doors. Other rooms are made up of nothing more than some thin dividers arranged around a massage table with a curtain for a door.

For an oil massage in a Chinese massage parlor it is normal for the customer to get naked. Some customers who were fearful or nervous and left their underwear on have been told to remove them even at so called legitimate massage places. That's because it is difficult to do an oil massage on a customer wearing underwear.

Most regulars at happy ending massage parlors say they get naked and sit down waiting for their masseuse to return though others report covering themselves up with a towel. The idea some have is that customers who show they are comfortable in the nude put the masseuses at ease and lessen any idea that the customers may in fact be cops.

In any event after the masseuse enters the room the customer is told to lay down face first on the table. Their body is then covered up in a towel. The towel is moved around as the massage progresses but is normally not totally removed from the body until much later.

As mentioned, massages at Chinese massage parlors are typically done with the use of oil. Some customers don't want to be covered in oil. They have different reasons for this. Some don't want to be oiled up if they can't shower afterwards. Some fear that suspicious significant others will notice the oil on their bodies. Some simply find it uncomfortable. Normally customers can request that a massage be done without oil but in that case it is a lot less comfortable. In some cases a sort of talcum powder can be used instead of oil.

With or without oil the masseuses often ask customers if they want a hard or soft massage with their limited English. A hard massage involves varying amounts of pressure being applied to the back, buttocks and legs. A soft massage usually means the masseuse will lightly run her fingers over the body, giving the customer goosebumps and quite possibly getting him erect. Customers focused on getting a happy ending will usually ask for a soft massage if given the option. The idea behind that is that soft massage is more likely to lead to a happy ending. That's why people on websites about massage parlors often refer to a happy ending as "soft touch" when they write reviews.

Some who frequent Chinese massage parlors report that they will try to touch their masseuses lightly on the leg during their massages. According to them the masseuses will pull away if extras are not available or stay put if they are. I don't think there's much validity to this. In any case it sounds quite creepy.

I have no way to know for sure but I would imagine that most masseuses would much prefer that customers simply try to strike up a conversation with them. They would probably appreciate it and even be happy to be able to practice their English and get a break from the monotony of rubbing the backs of semi-sleeping guys day after day.

During the massage things will often get a bit sexy at least from the point of view of the customer. When the masseuse is rubbing legs, buttocks and thighs customers often get turned on. This doesn't seem to be much of a problem even for places that don't offer extras.

Since erections can be totally involuntary during a massage they are often ignored. On the other hand customers who maintain an erection for a sustained period of time are probably more likely to be noticed.

At some point during any massage customers are asked to flip over and lie on their back. That's where things can get iffy though it all becomes clear soon enough.

So, after getting their legs and backsides rubbed customers will sometimes be erect. Flipping over and having the towel moved makes that very obvious. Sometimes a masseuse will ask the question "do you want to turn over?" For guys in the know that itself can be an offer for extras. More usually the masseuse just says "turn over" or "flip" and starts rubbing the inside of the legs. Eventually, if extras are offered, the masseuse will move closer to the penis and balls. They may even tease the groin or go as far as grabbing the stick or nuts. At that point they will either move directly to performing a hand job or they will ask the customer questions like "do you want anything else?," or make a hand motion signaling a hand job and ask "okay?"

At most Chinese massage places in America where extras are on offer prices are not discussed before hand. When prices are discussed up front it is often a sign of poor services to come although there are exception. In any case, hand job happy endings can range from fast and mechanical to slow, oily and erotic. No matter the style of service customers nearly always get emptied out sooner rather than later.

During a happy ending at a Chinese massage parlor the masseuse may get topless or even naked but this is usually not the case. Some regulars find that they can gain more access to their masseuses if they visit repeatedly and offer to tip more once the service is already underway.

Most masseuses do seem to be okay with customers touching them over their clothes during a happy ending hand job but some are not. Since it's all a gray area there are no hard and fast rules. Ultimately the easiest way for anyone to get consent is usually to ask for it but human interactions can be complicated.

At the completion of a happy ending customers are usually cleaned up by the masseuse with either tissues or warm wet towels. After that the masseuse leaves the room. Customers them get dressed and head out to the front desk to pay. At around the same time customer give their masseuses a tip directly for their services. In a few cases when the owners of a place are unaware of extra services being offered, or at least pretend to be unaware, masseuses sometimes request that their tips be given discreetly in the privacy of the room.

Again there aren't any hard and fast rules but generally speaking the normal tip for a hand job at a Chinese massage parlor in the United States is around forty dollars. Obviously some guys give more. A few may even give less but they are less likely to receive good or even any service if they return. At times masseuses will come right out and ask for a certain amount and it is sometimes more than forty dollars.

Again, not every Chinese masseuse does happy endings! If at the end of a massage the masseuse simply says "okay that's it" and leaves the room, that means extras aren't being offered. Guys who explore massage parlors in an attempt to find places that offer happy ending accept that possibility. That's part of their fun. The standard tip at places that do not offer happy endings is around ten dollars.

After a customer becomes familiar with a Chinese massage place that offers extra services they often return. Once they are known they are more likely to get the services they are looking for with far less uncertainty. They may may opt for a 30 minute massage if the happy ending is all they're after. In that case the tip remains the same. They may also inquire about four and even six handed massages which ads another masseuse or two to the mix. That is available at many Chinese massage parlors that offer extras and even some that don't. Obviously each masseuse involved expects to be tipped for any many handed massage.

Earlier I alluded to fly by night Chinese massage places set up in houses and apartments. In the past these less common set ups could be found in listings in the backs of alternative papers. Later the ads migrated to the internet. They are usually short and to the point, saying things like "Asian massage, 555-555-5555."

Since these places are private and often located in residential areas where business is not technically allowed customers have to call ahead to make an appointment and get directions. These spots are discreet. Customers sometimes have to call two or even three times to gain admission. Then they are let inside only to have one or two doors locked behind them.

Once inside, customers typical receive a half-assed massage and then are asked what else they want. Hand jobs are standard services offered in these kinds of places but sometimes customers will be offered oral sex.

Some of the women will perform oral sex without protection, especially if they're older, but others require it even if its not effective. Customers who don't bring their own condoms will sometimes find masseuses in these places doing something strange like covering the penis in plastic wrap before popping it in their mouth.

Guys who become regular and trusted visitors of these places can be offered full service by women who get to know them or take a liking to them. The women who perform full service obviously do it because they can get more money but there are cases when they simply want to get some enjoyment for themselves and take the opportunity of using a trusted guy to get off on.

In these places prices will normally be negotiated up front. Customers may pay 40 dollars for an hour massage then negotiate other costs for further services. Sometimes customers can get away with paying a lot less than they would pay at a "normal" Chinese jack shack like those described above.

I am aware of at least one place were the sexy middle-aged Chinese manager also did massages herself. She got really into her work and went above and beyond the call of duty. She'd jerk and blow customers with her big boobs out without even asking for a tip! At forty dollars a go all included it was quite a bargain in comparison to the competition. Of course it didn't last. These places never last. That's something regular customers are aware of.

As you should be able to tell from reading this, things are widely variable with Chinese massage parlors. Fans of the places usually have laid back attitudes and simply go with whatever comes.

Next I'll write about Korean massage parlors which have more straight forward and set-in-stone routines. In those massage parlors full service is more or less standard. Again all of this only applies to a certain subset of places and even those are only located in the United States. Things are much different elsewhere in the world, which I'll explain further on in the book.

Chinese Massage Parlors

Korean massage parlors differ from the Chinese variety of massage parlors in several ways. The main thing that sets them apart is the type of services offered. With few exceptions, Korean massage parlors offer full service, which of course is a euphemism for intercourse.

A table shower, which involves the customer laying on a covered massage table while being soaped up and rinsed by a masseuse, is also standard. That's a bonus both for the client and the woman servicing him who doesn't have to deal with any unnecessary body odors.

How can you tell if a massage parlor is Chinese or Korean? For those who know the difference between the Chinese and Korean people and their languages this is very easy. For others there are a number of clues that stand out.

Do customers have to call the place to find out the location? There's a good chance it's Korean. Is it open 24 hours or at least very late? There's a good chance it's Korean. Does the massage parlor or "spa" have a website with pictures of the girls who work there scantly clad in modeling poses? Then it's most likely Korean. Does it have all of the features above? Then it's most likely a Korean place. Online scouting can also indicate which places are Korean rather than Chinese. There are now numerous sites where people share information on Asian massage parlors in the US on a regular basis.

How do people find Korean massage parlors? There was a time when potential customers were limited to word of mouth and looking around town unless they could get their hands on alternative newspapers. The Yellow Pages were even an option back then. Some places had big ads placed under "massage." Today guys looking for Korean massage parlors typically seek out specific massage review websites out there like Rub Maps.

Obviously when I talk about "Korean massage parlors" I am not saying every massage parlor owned or staffed by Koreans operates in this way. That is definitely not the case. I am simply describing a particular category of adult oriented massage parlor that exists in the United States.

Korean massage parlors exist in most major cities and to a much lesser extent in some small towns. The prices and services are pretty much standard. In New York and other large cities customers typically pay $200 US dollars all in. In some smaller cities they'll pay 160 or 180. Guys who act like they don't know whats going on may be asked for a lot more. It's pretty rare for a customer to be ripped off in a Korean massage parlor even if they are a complete newbie but it does happen. Customers who are knowledgeable and prepared typically don't deal with that issue at all.

When guys visit a Korean massage parlor for the first time they usually call ahead to make an appointment or at least see if there is any availability. With a lot of places that is a necessity since the massage parlors don't list their exact locations in ads or on websites.

Customers usually need to call from an unblocked number. A lot of Korean massage parlors won't answer phone calls from private numbers. In the US cheap prepaid phones are easy to get and guys with discretion issues usually come up with a fake name. Nowadays there are even apps that let people temporarily use a phone number then discard it. So there are a lot of guys with names like "Joe" and "Frank" calling from burner phones and numbers that disappear from one day to the next.

In select big cities like New York a lot of Korean massage parlors have websites that feature pictures of the women on staff. When guys find a particular woman on a parlor's website attractive they can ask to set an appointment with her. In smaller cities that's a lot less common. Even where websites are available they don't always reflect reality.

In any event customers usually call ahead before visiting a Korean massage parlor. If they are regular visitors or the place has a more stable and well advertised location customers also have the option of just dropping in unannounced though they then run the risk of being turned away at the door.

When customers arrive at a Korean massage parlor they usually need to ring a doorbell. Most Korean massage parlors have secure steel doors with several locks in front. They also tend to have video cameras above the door so they can see who is outside before they open their doors. This is meant to keep out unwanted "surprise visitors" like robbers or other more devious creatures from simply stopping by. Customers typically arrive alone and are able to gain entrance by smiling at the camera and waiting.

New customers at any Korean massage parlor are usually asked if they have been there before. Lying in these places often doesn't work because unlike the massage girls the managers, often called mamasans, tend to stick around for a while and have good memories. In some cases they even keep record books with names and numbers of customers that they share with other managers to block out undesirable customers. Educated guys who want to enter a Korean massage parlor for the first time usually say that they have been to other parlors before and have decided to try a new location. Or they simply say that a friend recommended the place. Of course guys aren't necessarily turned away if they just say "no, I haven't." It depends on the situation.

After gaining entrance to a Korean massage parlor customers are led into a private room. Sometimes the manager will do the leading. At other times a masseuse will. The masseuses in the Korean massage parlors are most often more attractive than those at the Chinese parlors. They are usually dressed in a revealing nightie or other sexy garb too.

The Korean women who work in the Korean massage parlors usually come to the United States as visitors or live there permanently and rotate around any number of parlors. They normally don't stay in any one place too long though some do maintain permanent homes.

In the bigger cities, they staff at Korean massage parlors are typically made up of very attractive women in their twenties and thirties. Quite often they have well shaped large fake breasts and nice hair and makeup. In the smaller cities the women working the Korean massage parlors will usually be less attractive and often older gals that have aged out of the big city scene. They are still attractive enough in most cases and are commonly very skilled at their jobs. At one time these were the hotties in their twenties working in New York and Los Angeles. In some rare cases especially in more rural areas some of the women working in Korean massage parlors are at the end of middle age or older. Surprisingly they still do get customers. If they didn't they wouldn't be in the game.

Customers usually pay either the mamasan upon entry or the massage gal as soon as they get into the room. The standard rate is 60 per hour though it may be more in some places. Shops may offer a half hour session or they may not but guys in the know always opt for the hour to show that they're serious. They are also prepared and pay in cash. This money goes to the house.

Customers also have to pay for the extras. In New York and perhaps some other of the biggest cities the standard rate for full service is between 140 and 160 dollars and has been that way for some time. In the rest of the United States it varies between 100 and 140 on top of the house fee. All together the rates for service at a Korean massage parlor in America range from $160 to 220 USD.

Either immediately after asking for the house payment or a few minutes into the pathetic excuse for a massage that's provided customers will usually be asked what they want. In some places the masseuses will offer first timers lesser action like a hand job or blow job. This seems to be a way of testing new customers out. On repeat visits the same customers are sometimes offered full service. More commonly though it is simply expected that customers are looking for full service and so they are charged accordingly with no questions asked.

Korean massage parlor regulars tend to simply hand over the total amount together with the house fee all at once to show that they know the deal and are ready for action. Guys who opt for a hand job or blow job have to negotiate their own rates. They won't pay more than the going rate for full service.

When customers make appointments with a specific girl then that girl tends to be the service provider they get. When guys don't request a particular woman they are given whoever is next in rotation. Some experienced customers will ask for a "lineup" of available women to choose from though this is considered bad form. It is a common practice in Korea but the Koreans working in the United States don't seem to like it much. There are reasons these women work in the US to begin with. Since they often refuse to service Korean customers all together it seems that one of their motivations may be to get away from particular types of customers.

Korean massage parlors are usually clean and neat. The rooms are always private with complete walls that go up to the ceiling and locking doors. Some of the parlors are subdivided with thin walls so customers can hear what's going on outside of their rooms to some small extent but guys won't run into any paper walls or curtain "doors" like they'll find in some Chinese parlors.

Upon entering a private room customers are told to take off their clothes and wait. Sometimes the masseuse will stay in the room to watch or help the customer get undressed. Other times they will leave for a few minutes. When the customer tenders payment the girl will leave the room to give it to the house mom. Sometimes this is all combined into one action when a masseuse says something like "please give me the money and get undressed." In any case the customers simply sit tight and wait for their service providers to return.

Some Korean massage parlors give customers clear plastic pouches for their phones and wallets. This is so those valuables can be carried into the table shower and sauna. That ensures that nothing is stolen and that no one can pretend anything was taken either.

After taking off their clothes customers are normally given a towel. Experienced guys sometimes make sure their masseuse sees them naked before wrapping the towel around their body if they are at a new place. This is intended to let the service provider know what she's working with and help relax her a little bit keeping in mind they have a large number of things to worry about from customers who just walk in off the street. The thinking is that if the guy is cool she will be more likely to be too.

After undressing, customers will either be offered a table shower or simply led to a wash room. They put on the provided slippers and follow their masseuses to be bathed. Korean massage parlors are great at discretion and organization. Although a guy might hear another customer enter he will probably never ever actually see one inside.

Once customers enter the shower room they disrobe and wait for the masseuse to spray some warm water on a big table specially designed for table showers. If a customer lays on the table before it's prepared he'll not only look like a newbie he'll also run the risk of freezing his nuts off!

After the table has been cleaned and prepared customers are told to lay down face first on the table. This is typically the time the service providers feel out their customers. As they lather up the clients they may get into some small talk. The nicer the guys are during the table shower the better chance they have at getting superior service later.

After the service providers wash the customers from head to toe–including the butt hole–thoroughly, they say "turn over" and start to wash the front. Sometimes they will get playful when they wash the cock and balls but other times they will not. Guys who get hard at this point may give the kind of signal the masseuse is looking for but even those who stay limp are likely to get similar service since they've already gone far enough for most service providers to be comfortable. In addition, when experienced customers are offered mouthwash they take it. That may mean they're going to be allowed to kiss or do more later. Any customers who refuse mouthwash when offered run the risk of being refused themselves.

Once customer are washed and dried they are either led to a small sauna room or directly back to the private massage room. Sometimes the service providers ask if the customers want to use the sauna. If a Korean massage parlor is particularly busy sometimes they will put the customer in a steam room for storage while they do some work in another room. Customers who do end up in the sauna simply wait there until their masseuses return.

Back in the private rooms the customers are given a perfunctory massage. Experienced guys know not to expect any pain relief here at all. It's almost unheard of to get a decent massage in a Korean parlor. But that's not why guys visit them. Sometimes a customer will get nothing more than a few seconds of "soft massage" which involves the masseuse gently gliding her fingers on the customer's skin to get him relaxed and in the mood. Sometimes the service providers will do a few minutes of half-assed massage. And sometimes they'll get right to work with the sexual services.

If they didn't get their work supplies while the customer was in the sauna the masseuses will often leave at this point to retrieve them. They all have small bags containing lube and condoms that they use with their clients.

Once the massage ends and the supplies are retrieved

customers are told to lie down on the massage table on their backs. A lot of times the more professional girls will already have filled their pussies with lubricant so as not to ruin the mood.

Customers may get a cat bath which involves being licked all over with a special concentration on the nipples and balls. Sometimes the anus is also orally stimulated. This is all popular and common in Asia. It appears in varying degrees in Korean massage parlors in America.

The service providers then get their customers hard and apply a condom usually by using their mouth. Most of the service providers at Korean massage parlors are very good at this. More than one man has expressed his amazement at their ability to get hard instantly in these situations when they previously suffered from what was labeled erectile dysfunction. Many have also voiced amazement over the ability of some Korean service providers to apply a condom by mouth in a way that left them wondering if a condom was ever put on at all.

Korean service providers working in massage parlors typically use Asian condoms that are very thin and very high quality. They apply these then perform oral sex for a varying amount of time. Some will suck their customer and work his nuts with their hands for quite a while. Some will only give a few mechanical up and down oral motions.

One woman who worked at a shop in the Midwest used to do her best to make customers blow their loads early on with her "magic mouth". Those are her words, not mine. She wasn't very attractive. She had an older worn face and big, badly installed bolt-on tits. I'm sure most of her customers did not mind finishing by fellatio. Experienced customers who come close to cumming with hotter girls early on when things are still in the oral stage would probably be more likely to ask to slow down so there would be an opportunity for vaginal intercourse if they were dealing with someone other than old magic mouth.

As the main event unfolds the masseuses climb on top of their customers and start riding. Customers who want to go down on a service provider have to ask for that before the bucking begins. I can't be sure but I would guess that most customers skip the cunnilingus and get right in the routine. That would explain why the service providers normally go from blowing to humping. One thing to note is that while requests for oral either way are usually accepted, vaginal fingering is normally not permitted.

Once the full service begins some providers will allow all kinds of roaming hands and kissing. Others are princess-like and want none of it. Some treat their tits like prize possessions and will shy away from even nipple licking by customers. Others will let the customer have at it. Guys in the know just go with the flow, as they even tend to find their "bad" experiences in these places quite enjoyable.

If customers don't shoot their wad while they are being ridden things usually progress to missionary style. The transition typically involves the service provider climbing down, laying on her back and spreading her legs wide and invitingly.

The service providers are usually quite good at holding their customers back with their legs and arms in what feels like an embrace. In fact this maneuver is really meant to keep the customers from going in them too hard and deep. Considerate and caring guys are most appreciated by service providers since they can control themselves instead of being controlled. At the end of the day sex is a job for the women working these places. They want to avoid undue stress on themselves and their private parts.

Customers will usually only be given doggy style access if they directly request it during sex. If they do that they still may be denied though they usually are not. Guys who go crazy and start pounding away are by all accounts not warmly received. Many of the service providers who work at massage parlors are rather tight in the vaginal region even though they bang guys on a regular basis. They don't want to ruin the goods that they use to make a living or feel pain. Considerate guys along with any person with a functioning brain can understand this.

After customers shoot their loads the service providers grab their junk by the base and pull it out ensuring that the rubber stays on and no seed is spilled. Then the service providers gently remove the condom and put a wet towel over the still pulsating penis. As the customers kick back and relax the providers leave the room and come back with a warm wet towel to gently clean things up.

Most sessions wind up with some small talk. The service providers usually help their customers get dressed too. Mileage will vary here even with the same girl. Sometimes they want to lie together and cuddle with customers and sometimes they want to get the guy out the door as soon as possible. A customer may be thanked and offered a drink or candy by the mamasan on the way out, or he may not see anything but the door. Generally speaking the nicer customers are more likely to receive better service in the future.

It really is as simple as that. A guy makes an appointment, goes in, has a good time with a hot girl, and then leaves. That's one of the reason these places are so common and popular.

As it stands Korean massage parlors tend to be some of the most reliable adult oriented shops in the country. On top of that they often employ some of the most attractive women of any business of their kind. That doesn't seem set to change anytime soon despite the wishes of some in the anti-sex brigade.

These are general overviews and not iron clad rules. There are always exceptions. On top of the many legitimate massage parlors owned by Koreans or Chinese people where no sexual service are offered, there are also other types of venues around.

For example, in a few locations Korean owned massage parlors may only offer the same kind of hands-on extras most common to Chinese shops, or something more exotic like the soapy body slide. There are also Chinese owned massage parlors where full sex is offered to customers.

Of course things are much different elsewhere in the world and in other kinds of happy ending massage shops.

Russian Massage Parlors

Russian massage parlors in the United States aren't nearly as common as their Chinese or Korean counterparts, but where they exist they are pretty straightforward about the services they offer. These shops mainly seem to exist in New York and the Philadelphia area, but I have also seen a few elsewhere.

It's not too tough to figure out whether or not a place is Russian. For one, they usually advertise as such. Even when they don't, it doesn't take a whole lot of brain power to figure out that a place staffed with blond women with names like Svetlana and Olga who speak accented English is probably Russian.

Russian massage parlors may also employ women from the sphere of the former Soviet Union. That means that Belorussian, Kazakh, Ukrainian, and women from a host of other areas may be the ones giving customers their "Russian" rub downs. While the nationalities of the masseuses has little bearing on the services provided it does still seem to be in some way relevant to any report on the subject.

Russian massage parlors in the United States are somewhat rare and little seen. Besides being few and far between, they typically stick to advertising through select avenues and are less likely to appear on review websites.

At the same time, many Russian massage parlors are oriented to sexual services almost completely. Some may even describe them as being closer to brothels than massage shops.

Most Russian massage parlors of an adult nature require customers to make appointments before visiting. There's usually no other option especially for first time customers as the majority of these places do not even advertise their locations publicly.

The rates for sex at Russian massage parlors are usually between 160 and 200 US dollars. Customers looking to pay for such activities normally book a one hour session on their first visit. They then hand over all of the money for the sessions which is normally all that is required by the provider. Some customers do tip on top of the standard fee but the shops themselves don't usually require any additional payment. There are a select few Russian places that ask customers to pay a house fee of something like 50 dollars up front with customers left to negotiate the rest of the payment with the providers in private but even then the total cost usually amounts to about the same 160 to 200 dollars.

Russian massage parlors operate a lot like Korean massage parlors, and also tend to staff attractive women in their early-twenties to mid-thirties. Breast implants are a lot less common at Russian places than Korean places but some providers do sport silicone. At Russian massage parlors showers before and after sessions are sometimes required and sometimes not available at all. Sessions usually start with a very brief, mediocre rubdown and then quickly proceed into sexual activity.

The level of performance at Russian massage parlors seems to be a bit lower than what customers normally get in Korean massage parlors, but there are big exceptions. Some of the women working in these Russian establishments either get really into it or otherwise deserve Academy Awards for their acting abilities. When no tip is expected these over the top performances can only really be explained by enthusiasm or a wish by providers to satisfy their customers.

Another difference between Korean and Russian massage parlors is the question of oral sex. While the majority of women in Russian massage parlors do perform oral sex on their customers, there are some who do not.

Since oral sex is not something most first time customers or providers can bring up safely it is often not discussed upfront. Because of that customers only find out whether or not oral sex is offered at a particular place or by a specific provider when they go through an actual session. Whether or not oral sex is provided the majority of sessions end up the same way, with condom covered full service.

It should be noted that some of the Russian operations, especially when set up hastily, are basically rip off joints. While there are some no-happy-endings-allowed Chinese massage parlors that try to attract horned up men by running ads containing pictures of sexy Asian models in media outlets where erotic services usually appear, this sort of bait and switch does seem to be more common with Russian places.

Russian massage parlors with no reviews appearing anywhere online would be most likely to do the bait and switch. Guys looking for sexual services in these places may keep upping their tips in the vein hopes of getting something but end up with little more than an expensive back rub. It is not necessarily common, but it's not unheard of either.

American Massage Parlors

American massage parlors are probably the most common massage shops after Chinese massage parlors in the United States.

It is widely known that the regular mainstream massage chains with witless names offer nothing more than body rubs that purport to be therapeutic. But what about the independent massage parlors with names like "Hollywood Massage" and staffs that range from cosmopolitan mixes to those more uniformly white than North Dakota in January?

Well in some cases, those types of places may very well be shady shops that are little more than knocking shops in disguise. In other cases they may be upstanding shops with pristine walls decorated with licenses and training certificates in the front and a row of tanning beds set up somewhere in the back. Most fall somewhere in between.

There really is no standard when it comes to these kinds of massage parlors. They may offer hands on happy endings, full service, or nothing extra whatsoever. Services may even differ between individual masseuses in a particular shop. An official prohibition against extra sexual services from the management doesn't stop a lot of women from offering them in private as a way to make extra money.

In some American massage shops happy endings simply don't happen, but aroused guys are invited to finish themselves off. They may even be offered this fantastic "bonus" if, and only if, they promise to tip generously. Some customers enjoy this or are at least able to settle for such limited services. Others look to other venues for more with the idea that they can masturbate themselves at home without spending a dime.

Because of the wide variation that exists between shops and even individual providers I can't give any real average price points for these kinds of American massage parlors. I can say that they tend to ask for higher rates than the women who work in Asian and Russian massage parlors and offer comparable services. Why is that? Perhaps the native-born women who work American massage parlors feel more entitled. Perhaps they are conditioned to expect more by growing up in the richest country in the world. Maybe it's a combination of the two, or not related to either. Who knows?

Some happy ending massage aficionados in the United States swear by American massage parlors that offer extras. Others avoid them all at all costs sticking to places like Korean and Chinese massage parlors instead.

Most of the customers for these American massage places are probably irregular visitors who either wander in or hear or read something that intrigues them.

Thai, Tantric and Other Massage

Over the last several pages I've covered the most common types of massage shops in the United States, but what about the rest? I needn't make any mention of hair salons and "legitimate" spas that offer therapeutic massage services. It should be obvious that they typically don't offer extra services of any kind. I'll discuss here the other types of massage venues and providers in the US that may offer happy endings.

After the Chinese, Korean, American and Russian massage parlors, the next most prominent has to be the Thai massage parlor. These places seem to be a lot more common on the West Coast, though they do exist elsewhere. I'm not talking about the American massage shops that may list "Thai massage" as one of their service specialties. I'm speaking of the Thai massage parlors that are owned and operated by Thai people.

Actual Thai massage is a form of reflexology that developed in the country it is named after many years ago. While in Thailand the women working in many massage parlors offer at least some form of happy ending if requested, in the United States the Thai massage parlors seem to tend more toward the "legitimate" side of things. There are no hard and firm rules when it comes to Thai massage parlors. Prices and services vary a lot from one shop to another. For that reason the guys who seek out happy ending massage in these sorts of places usually rely heavily on user reviews they find online or even word of mouth.

In some ways the typical Thai massage parlor in the US will operate like the Chinese massage parlors described earlier. The main difference is that customers will often be asked to put on a sort of silky pajama set before their massage. Another difference is that happy endings are probably a lot more rare in

Thai massage parlors with a few notable exceptions.

Beyond the Thai massage parlors there are a few other ethnically based places around, usually focused around the neighborhoods where people of those ethnicities live.

Latina massage exists in the form of a handful of massage parlors and temporary setups in residential and office buildings scattered throughout major cities. These are usually established by either Chinese or Latino owners and advertised alongside other similar facilities on websites and in the back of newspapers. Advertisements sometimes even appear in Spanish.

I have never heard of a Latina massage shop that didn't offer extras of some form or another, but I'm quite sure such mainstream massage parlors staffed exclusively by Latinas do exist most probably in heavily Latino areas.

Some Latina massage places will offer a bit of perfunctory massage, but in many others the service providers get straight down to business. Rates range from the incredibly inexpensive to the same amounts typically charged in a Korean or Russian facility. Otherwise things don't differ radically from most other massage parlors described above with the exception of the types of women on staff.

Vietnamese massage parlors are another example of "other" ethnic massage parlors that exist in the United States. They aren't plentiful, and like the secretive Vietnamese cafes and hair salons that staff women who can sometimes offer sexual services, they can be difficult to impossible for outsiders to figure out or even gain access to. Things are different in Vietnam. In the US guys who don't speak Vietnamese or at least have a Vietnamese friend to vouch for them are unlikely to see the inside of any of these places.

Greek, Turkish and Russian spas are normally not places where any kind of happy ending service is served up. In some cases male customers go to these places to get intense therapeutic massages from other men. Other times they are places where guys search out other men to have anonymous sex with. Happy endings from women aren't offered.

Tantric massage practitioners offer the surest bet willing customers to get a happy ending massage, though they often have to put up with a healthy does of new age mumbo-jumbo. The ideas behind tantric massage are a mix of various forms of traditional and modern spirituality that are well beyond the scope and subject of this book. In essence, guys who go in for a tantric massage normally receive a very effective and relaxing massage that will often involve at least one orgasm, though sometimes they are restricted to the so-called "dry orgasm" promoted by some that stops short of causing actual ejaculation.

Originating in India quite some time ago, Tantric massage emerged in North America in the 1960's and 70's. Today, it is usually on offer in the biggest cities where it is most often practiced by independent individuals or groups of two in small spaces and private homes. Some tantric masseuses will also travel to the homes or hotels of their customers. Tantric practitioners advertise in all sorts of places, often right alongside more mainstream masseuses who may or may not scorn the idea of tantra all together.

Tantric practitioners often utilize their own detailed websites to find new customers too. A quick Google search can bring up countless tantric masseuses.

It should be noted that tantric massage providers usually do not appear on review websites that list massage parlors for whatever reason. Reviews can be found online on other kinds of websites however.

Tantric massage often involves things like music and candles, and a little bit of back and forth. The service provider, who may refer to herself by some Tantra jargon like "Dakini" rather than "masseuse," will normally try to tailor each session to the perceived needs of the client.

Customers of tantric masseuses can expect things like

breathing instruction and the like alongside the rubdown. Wraps and body scrubs may also be on the menu. Long, extended periods of erotic enjoyment will typically be included in the session even when it is billed as a sort of spiritual or even medical healing. The goal for tantric providers seems to be to prolong things. Depending on the customers, the session booked and the service provider, those undergoing a tantric massage might be brought to climax one or several times, or alternatively not at all.

Note that tantric massage practitioners take their craft and the philosophy behind it very seriously. Customers who visit tantric practitioners either have to play along with the whole ordeal or lay back in silence while enjoying the finer aspects of the art if they want to complete a session. Guys who show up to a tantric session talking about happy endings and blowing loads, or anything similar, are much more likely to be shown the door than a good time.

Tantric massage typically costs much more than any of the other happy ending massage options in the US. There is no set rate that applies across the board, but sessions often cost between 375 to 500 dollars an hour. Longer sessions are available, and recommended by practitioners, though the price continues to go up in correlation with the extension of time. The biggest advocates of tantric massage are known to suggest sessions of three hours or more though such appointments can cost more than a thousand bucks.

Unlike massage parlors where customers can book as little as an hour before a session or even just walk in, those who want a tantric massage typically need to make reservations much further in advance. Some tantric service providers even want to talk a bit or meet potential customers for an "introduction session" before agreeing to any booking. As might be expected, those who are more laid back and easy going are more likely to get the kinds of services they seek.

Couples and women looking for massage with release

find that nearly every tantric masseuse will gladly take them on as customers and provide the services they are looking for. The service is sometimes given a different name like "yoni massage" but the end result is the same.

There are also a few masseuses in the United States that operate under titles like "sexologist" or "sexual health instructor." They do things much in the same way as their self-proclaimed tantric counterparts except that may they work from a basis of education rather than spirituality. Still, rates and services can be very similar.

Masseuses who use terms like "sensual instructor" usually fall somewhere between the two.

For whatever reason, those who provide tantric massage, sensual instruction and like usually operate much more in the open than some of the other masseuses who provide extra services. My only guess is that since they base their practice on ideas of spirituality and education, they feel they are immune from laws designed to curb the sale sexual services.

Tantric massage may be more tolerated than other forms of sensual or sexual massage in the US because it couches itself in spiritual or holistic terms. This can be viewed as being something like head shops in the US that sell water pipes and the like. Customers who enter those places talking about marijuana are often refused service even though everyone more or less knows that no one smokes tobacco through a bong.

In any event the billing of tantra as a holistic practice seems to work. As far as I can tell, few are ever prosecuted for offering tantric massage or hands-on sexual instruction in the United States. The same can not be said for other erotic massage providers.

Traveling and Independent Masseuses

I would be remiss in a report like this if I did not also make mention of traveling or "outcall" masseuses in the United states. They may operate under any number of titles, and either as independent individuals or as staff members of larger organized operations. They tend to advertise in the same kinds of places as escorts, and there's a very good reason for that.

Most of the women advertising offers of outcall, erotic or sensual massage are simply selling full service sex. This may or may not be proceeded by an actual massage, but even when it is, the massage rendered isn't typically of the type that would offer much in the form of pain relief.

Some of these traveling ladies do not offer full service, or at least do not offer it in all situations. These masseuses are more likely to show up with folding massage tables and oils and consider their work to be more on the therapeutic than sexual side of things.

Guys who call traveling masseuses they find in ads and ask about things like extra sexual services or happy endings are usually not given the time of day. In what is a largely hostile world these traveling ladies put in a lot of effort to protect themselves.

Those men who actually expect to meet the women in question are usually much more demure and simply go with the flow of things rather than engaging in any explicit conversation.

Traveling masseuses who advertise alongside escorts and visit customers in their private residences or hotel rooms at all hours of the day and night often do offer sensual services.

Those who charge rates of 200 dollars or more per hour and more likely to offer full service than just happy endings by hand.

Masseuses who do outcall to customer's rooms and show up at one o'clock in the morning wearing revealing mini skirts with no massage supplies are probably most likely to be escorts who offer little or no massage at all.

I chose my words carefully when I say "most likely." You'll notice that I do not say anything about sureties or guarantees. If as they say there are no guarantees in life, there certainly aren't any when it comes to erotic massage.

Obviously, and to repeat what was written earlier in this book, these are generalities. There are absolutely mainstream masseuses who visit clients in their homes, charge high rates, and do not offer sensual or sexual services of any kind.

Guys who actively seek out erotic massage most often look for online reviews in advance of booking sessions with any kind of masseuse. That's especially true of the kinds of outcall masseuses described here who can be all over the place.

Even reviews can be off base. They can be mistaken or even based on outright lies. Service providers can also change or change their minds. No guy in his right mind would demand anything especially based on an anonymous online review though sadly some probably do. Experienced clients tend toward just relaxing and seeing what comes along even when something someone has said or written gives them an idea of what to expect. That's one way they avoid problems.

Traveling outcall masseuses sometimes ask customers to pay upfront, especially if they have experience with people not paying for their services. Even with that being the case experienced clients usually do not pay in advance or they place payment in a white envelope somewhere out in plain sight. The masseuses pick up this money on their way out of the rooms after sessions conclude. I don't know how this practice begin but I do know that it has become somewhat standard in the home erotic massage scene as well as among the very similar escorting scene that exists.

Outcall erotic masseuses are more likely than others to have one full set price that includes all their services though there are some who ask for tips for extras or do an upsell during their services to try to get more money. Masseuses who walk a thin line between straight ahead services and manipulation usually get poor reviews but still find no shortage of clients thank to the large number of guys looking for the kinds of services the ladies offer.

Masseuses who use terms like "licensed massage therapist" or "therapeutic massage and bodywork" in their advertisement are almost always completely and totally serious about therapeutic massage and totally adverse to offering any kinds of happy ending. There are some "legitimate" masseuses out there who do travel to homes, hotels and offices. Guys who try for sensual services with them can run into real trouble.

When hotels offer in-room massage services in the US, things are usually therapeutic and nothing more. In rare cases when any extra services are offered it is up to the discretion of the masseuse making the offer. No mainstream hotel in the United States is going to endorse the provision of happy endings. Those adventurous men who are able to score extra services in private hotel massages seem to do very delicately worded with the help of generous tips. Even those men are often rejected or worse. Erotic services are not commonly offered by house masseuses in hotel in the United States at all.

Why so much confusion and misdirection with all sorts of different erotic and mainstream therapeutic masseuses? The situation gives rise to it.

Because of the atmosphere that exists, those who do offer erotic massage often do not mention it or use round about language or codes to describe their work. Others rely on online reviews and word of mouth. Probably some regular mainstream masseuses get mixed up in it all too with confused guys thinking they offer sexual services.

Massage Parlor Advertisements

Advertisements for massage parlors and independent masseuses abound. They are most commonly found in the backs of alternative and ethnic newspapers and on websites related to the industry. Formerly they were also found on websites like Backpage and Craigslist until laws and decisions came into play that removed any option for massage ads.

It seems that Korean, Russian and American massage parlors, along with some independent masseuses, are the only advertisers who feature photographs of actual masseuses or service providers in their ads. Even then faces are often obscured for reasons that should make sense to pretty much everyone.

Other massage parlors are more likely to use images lifted off of the internet that bare little to no resemblance to anyone on staff. If the woman in the ad for a local Chinese massage parlor looks a lot like a Japanese adult model it's because she is one. She doesn't work at "Tao's Massage" in Albuquerque. She's a porn star from Tokyo who has no idea she even appears in such an ad.

Law enforcement agencies in the US have even been known to use massage parlors and masseuses as fronts to set up stings. They will post some sort of phony ad to attract unwitting guys to a location where they will be arrested for the crime of giving another adult an agreed upon sum of money in exchange for a hand job

Most regular happy ending massage clients consider massage parlor review websites and internet forums that are fueled by the contributions of active customers to be the most trusted sources for information on the industry.

Still others stick to themselves and base their activities on nothing more than their own experiences and intuition.

Massage Outside of the United States

This book has thus far focused on erotic and sensual massage in the United States of America. There are a few reasons for this. One is that a lot of English speaking book reading men live or originate there. Secondly, I have written extensively about the sexual services available around the world online and in other books. The third and final reason is that, in many of the countries of the world, it is incredibly easy to get a happy ending massage with the practice either being completely acceptable or otherwise unofficially permitted. In such places a report almost seems redundant even though I never think the quest for knowledge or entertainment is futile.

With all of that said I will spend some time reporting on the wide variety of happy ending massage options commonly offered outside of the United States in the pages that follow. In order to stay on task, I will give a brief overview of some of what's out there in the wide world.

Canada, Australia, New Zealand

In places like Canada, Australia and New Zealand, massage parlors are perfectly within their legal rights to offer happy endings. Prices and procedures are pretty similar to massage parlors in the United States, with all sorts of Chinese, Korean and local massage parlors in existence. With full service often available from escorts and brothels in the immediate area, these places tend to stick to other services like hand relief, oral relief and sumata. For those unaware, sumata is a type of simulated sex that involves a masseuse straddling a customer and working his unit with her lubricated hands and inner thighs in a way that makes the client feel as if he is actually having unprotected sexual intercourse.

There are massage parlors and individual masseuses who offer full service sex in all of these countries but they do not predominate.

Thailand

Thailand is dotted with massage parlors from one side of the country to the other. Some facilities are targeted at locals others at the millions of expats and foreign visitors the country receives each year.

Massage places like the soapies, oilies and nuru massage shops are designed to be little more than brothels with massage preludes. These are quite common, and they exist alongside countless over options for sexual services.

Soapy massage parlors are large complexes that resemble big hotels. Inside they typically have a "fishbowl" setup that with several women sitting on bleacher type seating behind glass. Customers select the women by number and go to a private room which is typically big and well decorated. In the rooms there are big bath tubs that can fit two or more people along with a big bed. In some soapies the rooms also contain inflatable mattresses. The women get fully nude and cover themselves and these mattresses with soapy water then slide against their customer's bodies, hence the name "soapy massage parlor." The soapy body slide service isn't as common as you might think, but full service sex is on the menu in basically every soapy massage parlors. Charges typically range from 1300 to 7000 Baht ($39-210 USD).

Oily massage parlors are basically standard massage parlors that double as brothels. They tend to look like massage parlors but they have more scantly clad women inside or even menus explicitly explaining what they offer. There are more oily massage parlors in Bangkok than any other part of the country with large concentrations on streets like Sukhumvit Soi 24/1.

Prices are pretty uniform across the oily massage parlors. The standard is for a one hour session that includes mutual showering and full sex at around 2000 Baht ($60 USD) all in.

There are other types of erotic massage places around including kinky massage parlors and nuru massage parlors which offer a body to body slide similar to the aforementioned soapies. Their prices and layouts can differ greatly. In Chiang Mai there are several massage places around that cater to locals but accept foreigners too. They often offer hand job happy endings from university students or part time amateurs. In Pattaya there are cheaper places with smaller and usually worse rooms that are basically brothels concentrated on streets like Soi Honey.

The many Thai massage places found all over the country that look more like the massage shops you'd see in the United States offer "legitimate" massage to men and women, but many masseuses who work in them are open to offering hand relief to customers at the very least for the right tip. Men are often offered such services without solicitation in these sorts of places. Thai massages and oil massages usually cost between 150 and 300 Baht. Tips for extras start at 500 Baht and are negotiated between providers and their customers.

Cambodia

Outside of Thailand, Cambodia probably has a higher number of massage parlors per person than any other country in the world. Massage parlors of varying types are literally spread all over the country. They're especially common in the capital city of Phnom Penh.

Of all the various massage setups in Cambodia there are basically a few types of places were happy ending massage is typically offered.

First there are the mainstream style massage parlors. Usually these places look like the standard Thai massage parlors in Thailand. They offer services like oil massages for between $6 and $8 USD. There are many along the riverside in Phnom Penh and another large concentration along Sothearos Boulevard near Aeon Mall in the same city.

These places never offer happy ending massage as an open matter of course. It's not on any menus and normally not offered publicly either. But in private some of the masseuses will offer foreign customers sensual services in exchange for a tip. A few will even go beyond and offer additional services up to and including oral and even full sex.

The tips for these services are negotiated between the providers and their customers and can range from $5 to $50 dollars American. The services are rendered discreetly as the owners and managers of these places are often unaware such things go on.

Not every woman working in these kinds of places does hand jobs or more for money. I have no way to know what percentage of masseuses in these kinds of places offer sensual services but the practice certainly is not rare.

A second kind of place is the budget local massage parlor. These are very low end places that are usually made of rooms separated into sections by cardboard or thin wood. They have mattresses covered by sheets that don't appear to ever have been changed. A handful of women serves as the staff. They usually wait out front for customers.

Once these places all charged a uniform 5000 Riel, which is about $1.25 USD. Nowadays they charge anywhere from 5,000 to 10,000 Riel or even more. While these cheap massage parlors are common they are not necessarily conspicuous to the untrained eye.

Often the only indication that these places exist are wooden signs posted in front of the shops that say things like "massage" in the local Khmer language along with a posted price in Riel.

Some of these places actually double as brothels. Most are actually legitimate massage parlors however. Local guys typically enter for an actual massage. Adventurous foreigners are more likely to expect and receive other services when they wander in. The women on staff rarely speak English but they know how to negotiate prices for things like mechanical hand jobs delivered for tips ranging between $3 and $10 dollars.

Some massage places located in places like the Toul Tom Pong section of Phnom Penh or in the small seaside city of Kampot follow a similar model but are a bit nicer. They tend to operate out of shop houses and staff a small number of women. They can offer anything from a mediocre massage for a few dollars to full service for between ten and thirty bucks.

Another kind of budget massage parlor has recently emerged in Phnom Penh too, especially concentrated around areas like Streets 130, 136 and 172 where there a lot of foreign guys and even more hostess bars. Building on the aforementioned low cost massage parlors sometimes used by guys looking for more, these places set up shop by throwing a couple of mattresses on the ground, putting a couch in the lobby, and setting a sign out front that says something like "Massage $3."

The women who work these places are usually in their twenties and thirties and range in terms of looks and English skill. Some are aggressive and call out to foreign men in the street. Others lay back on the couches or floor playing with their phones indifferently.

These places seem to more or less operate like brothels with only pretenses of massages given in most cases. It should be noted that these sorts of places have a reputation for thievery, and there are many stories of customers including local guys being relieved of money from their pants while receiving massages!

The final form of massage parlor that commonly offers erotic services in Cambodia is the fishbowl type of massage shop.

These fishbowl massage parlors are the biggest and most sex based of all the massage parlors in the country. They operate more or less like the above described soapy massage parlors of Thailand except they don't have bathtubs and no one does a soapy slide.

Still, customers walk inside these places and look at the available service providers who sit waiting on bleacher type seats behind glass windows. After customers select one of the available women they pay a house fee which typically ranges from between $6 and $12 depending on the place.

Next customers move into a private room with their chosen service provider. These are normally large but sparsely decorated. They typically include things like a bed, a table and television but not much else.

After customers shower they sometimes receive a perfunctory massage before being asked if they'd like a "special massage" or "boom boom" which are ways of indicating that full service sex is on offer. Prices are negotiated between the service providers and range from as low as $20 to $100 USD.

Somewhat interestingly, the fishbowl massage parlors in Cambodia, which are mostly concentrated in Phnom Penh, seem to be much more popular with locals and Asian businessmen than Westerner tourists who often aren't even aware that such places even exist.

Vietnam

Massage parlors are not nearly as common in Vietnam as they are in Thailand or even Cambodia but they do abound.

Numerous hotels in Vietnam contain massage setups that can be used by men staying at the hotels but are more commonly visited by guys looking specifically for a body rub with extras.

The hotel based massage parlors are usually large and elaborate venues located on upper floor accessed by elevators. They have front desk staff who explain prices in terms of rooms. Massage in regular rooms can cost as little as 100,000 Dong ($4 USD) while a body rub in a VIP room can cost closer to 700,000 ($30 USD).

The regular rooms are exactly that while the VIP rooms are big and contain everything from large screen televisions to huge whirlpool baths and private steam rooms. Food and drink are also provided to those in the VIP quarters.

The women who work the hotel massage parlors are almost universally attractive and usually in their early to mid twenties. They wear sexy uniforms typically consisting of silky blouses and tight skirts.

At these hotel massage parlors customers typically get bathed and massaged before being asked about a hand job finale. Some providers ask for a tip at least equal to the cost of the room for such services while others just take whatever is given. In some cases oral is also offered at similar or slightly higher rates. Full service is rare. Customers pay their room fees and tips all together after service has concluded.

Maybe even more common are faux hair salons and barbershops that offer "face massage" or something similar.

There are plenty of mainstream places staffed with attractive women who offer nothing more than what's advertised, but there are also many more in the side streets and so on where a hand job, blow job or even full service is offered in the private of a booth or small room. Prices are usually 100,000 Dong for the room and 100,000 to 300,000 Dong more for the service provider.

There are also regular massage parlors in Vietnam especially in the areas that attract the most foreign visitors such as District 1 around Pham Ngu Lao and Bui Vien streets in Ho Chi Minh City.

Extra services are often offered by the providers in these places who can speak some English and are keyed in to the interests and desires of foreign visitors. Massages in these places are typically not much more expensive than in any other massage place but extras can be offered at rates that are comparably quite high. These places rely on unwitting foreigners who don't know local rates or compare the costs of things in Vietnam to the costs of things in whatever country they come from.

Laos

Bordering Thailand, Vietnam and Cambodia, one might expect that Laos would be full of happy ending massage parlors. While there is a fairly large commercial sex scene in the sleepy rural country, erotic massage is not all that common. It at least it is not as common as some may think.

There are basically two types of massage parlors where happy endings are commonly offered in Laos. The first type is the typical massage parlor like one might see in Thailand or Cambodia. The second is a more specialized erotic massage place.

In cities like Vientiane there are some massage parlors that resemble their counterparts in Thailand. That's fitting since most of the Thai massage parlors in Thailand are actually staffed by people from Isaan who speak the same language as the masseuses in Laos.

In these kinds of places the standard service is a standard massage. As is the case in Thailand and Cambodia, some masseuses take opportunities presented to them however and offer happy endings to foreign customers in exchange for larger tips.

Hand jobs are the most common happy endings delivered in these Lao massage parlors, but oral sex an even full service is not unheard of. The rates are negotiated between providers and their customers and can range from next to nothing to the equivalent of more than one hundred US dollars.

Specialized sex massage parlors are more keyed in to what horny male customers want. They are also a lot less common. There are probably only a handful in the entire country. They are typically attached to hotels with rooms that resemble the quarters in Cambodian fishbowl massage parlors. The women who work these places are more commonly ethnically Vietnamese than Lao. The women tend to be in their twenties or thirties.

Sessions in these places resemble those in Thai soapy massage parlors or Cambodian fishbowl places too. Customers are washed then receive oral sex followed by full service.

The prices are usually the equivalent of around 50 US dollars. Sometimes payment is even accepted in American or Thai money.

The Philippines

Massage parlors in particular parts of the Philippines have become well known for their sensual services. "Lingam" and "Yoni" massage are neo-tantric terms used to describe the massage of the penis and vagina respectively. These services have become so widespread and popular in Cebu that they are now included as parts of tour packages promoted to people from China, South Korea and Japan. The rates on these services are extremely reasonable and posted right out in the open. Still these places face only limited issues, most probably because they focus on tourists who spend money and couch themselves in holistic terms.

Somewhat surprisingly for a country with such a large and widespread commercial sex industry, there are not so many happy ending massage parlors outside of these pseudo-spiritual facilities.

Most mainstream massage parlors are exactly that, and offer nothing other than normal rub downs. In some cases individual providers may offer happy ending hand jobs or more but many massage parlors even in well known sex industry centers like Angeles City expressly prohibit any massaging of the genitals or similar services.

There are exceptions. Countless women walk P Burgos Street in the Makati section of Manila every night offering massage to foreign guys. Some wear uniforms and photo ID badges while others don only their street clothes.

Massages are offered either in nearby parlors or in the private hotel rooms of customers. Prices are usually 500 Pesos ($9.50 USD) for the massage. Once in private, many of the masseuses will offer more than just mechanical body rubs. Services commonly rendered include everything from hand jobs to full service though there are women who treat their job as something purely therapeutic and non sexual even though they search out customers in what is basically a red light district.

The many who do offer erotic services negotiate their rates with their customers. Some have been known to include extras with the 500 Pesos standard massage. Others ask up to 4000 Pesos ($75 USD) for full service.

Finally, there are some fishbowl type massage parlors that should be mentioned. They are not necessarily common, but they do exist. Quezon City is probably home to more of these places than any other part of the country.

Often attached to karaoke parlors, these fishbowl massage parlors operate in more or less the same way as the aforementioned fishbowl massage parlors in Cambodia. They staff dozens of women who are typically in their twenties.

Customers select women by number from a group of available providers. Then they head into a private room that can range from the bare to the high end. After receiving a perfunctory massage, customers are typically provided with oral sex and full service.

The house fees at these kinds of places range from 950 to 2500 Pesos ($18-$46 USD). On top of that, the service providers themselves normally request an additional payment of 1300 to 2000 Pesos ($24-38 USD) in the room for full service.

South Korea

As hinted at earlier, South Korea is home to some real erotic massage traditions. I have not mapped out the origins of erotic massage in the Republic of Korea but suffice it to say, there is no shortage of happy ending massage in the land of the morning calm.

First there are the infamous ANMA massage parlors which exist throughout the country. ANMA is a word brought over from the Chinese language that describes massage. In South Korea, places labeled ANMA (안마) are basically the local version of the Korea massage parlors in the US.

Just like the Korean massage parlors there usually isn't much in the way of massage going on inside ANMA massage parlors, in spite of the name. They are staffed by scantly clad women who range from the average to the absolutely stunning.

ANMA massage parlors serve a mostly local clientele. In fact, most will not even accept foreign customers. When customers enter they pay a fee of around 180,000 Won ($160 USD). After that they are led to a room with a massage table. Attached to each room is a large shower room with another massage table.

Sessions usually start with a table shower followed by oral sex and full service. Some places have more elaborate services that can include things like a masked woman on an elevator giving blow jobs to customers as they ascend toward private rooms.

Similar to the ANMA are many smaller massage parlors scattered around the country, with a notable concentration in the small island town of Unseo near the Incheon International Airport. These places are labeled as everything from "sports massage" to just "massage."

These places follow a similar format to ANMA massage parlors but usually have older and perhaps less attractive women on staff. They are also more likely to accept foreign customers. Prices are usually around 150,000 Won ($132 USD) and payment is expected in advance.

Finally, there are the men's relaxation type massage parlors. Some describe these as "massage rooms" even though they are are much larger than a room!

These places aren't usually marked off as happy ending massage parlors but in fact that's what they are. Labeled as things like spas, they usually have facilities like a locker room, a large shower room, a dining area, and individual private rooms where men receive massages.

Customers typically pay fees of around 130,000 Won up front at these places. After showering they're given a very thorough and skilled massage by an lady in her thirties or forties. That massage concludes with the masseuse rubbing the customer's balls and perineum in order to get him aroused for the next portion. Afterwards, a more attractive women in her twenties arrives, gets topless, and finishes the session with a hand job or oral sex. Jinju Massage in the Gangnam section of Seoul is a well known example of this sort of place.

Some may find it surprising, but parlors labeled "Thai massage" in South Korea usually do not offer any sensual services whatsoever. That's true even when they are staffed by Thai women and located alongside erotic massage parlors. This goes to show that common knowledge and stereotypes are often not based in reality.

Japan

Japan has probably the largest commercial sex industry in the world. In many cases it is even legal to sell sexual services. You might think that in such an environment there would be no need for happy ending massage. You be wrong.

One form of happy ending massage in Japan comes in the *estute* massage parlors. Common in places like the Gotanda section of Tokyo, these are massage parlors usually staffed by Korean or Chinese women that offer sexual intercourse for money.

Outside of soaplands which are apparently exempt, the sale of vaginal intercourse is illegal in Japan. So these gray and black market places spring up to offer sex to horny guys under the cover of massage. Some last surprisingly long while others are quickly shut down.

Next there are the Chinese and Thai massage parlors that operate legally but offer hand job happy endings and occasionally more in a discreet fashion. These places are typically located on the upper floors of buildings. They put massage signs on the street level to advertise. The signs often contain either a Thai flag or heavily edited pictures of sexy Asian women who probably have no idea their image is being used.

The Thai massage places are likely to offer a legitimate body massage followed by the offer of a hand job happy ending. The Chinese places typically employ older women who are more scantly clad. Services in the Chinese places often consist of things like table showers followed by perfunctory massages and concluding with hand jobs or more. Prices can range from

Next come the places oriented entirely toward a hand

job happy ending massage. These shops usually staff attractive women who are sometimes from countries like Thailand. They wear somewhat revealing clothing and offer packages that include things like bathing and hand job happy endings. They operate out in the open and seem to have no problems.

Two of the most well known places of this type are Asian Feeling and Asian Relax, both of which are located in the infamous Kabukicho section of Tokyo. Prices at those shops start at 9000 Yen ($81) for a massage and hand job, which is fairly typical.

Another somewhat common setup is the erotic massage delivery model. These places tend more than others to be totally above board, legal, and licensed.

Customers call these businesses for an appointment. They select one of the available service providers and set a time and place. Private homes, hotel rooms and love hotels are common venues for appointments.

The women employed by these businesses are usually attractive and skilled. Sessions typically involve bathing, a long high quality full body massage with both the customer and provider in the nude, a hand job or oral happy endings, and a final bit of bathing.

Tokyo Style is probably the most well known business of this kind and not only because it is one of the few adult businesses in Japan that happily accepts foreign customers. As the name would suggest Tokyo Style is located in Tokyo. Others companies like it operate in other parts of the country. Prices start at 27,000 Yen ($243 USD) and go up from there.

There are also some totally legitimate therapeutic massage parlors scattered all over Japan. Not every place is giving hand jobs even though it is a fairly common practice.

China

Massage parlors are widespread in mainland China and a large percentage of them include a hand finish happy ending as a standard part of the rub down for male customers. The laws covering these acts are incredibly vague. The issue is currently under discussion in China, with things actually pointing in the direction of full legalization of massage parlors that offer only hand relief. If this plays out the famously repressive People's Republic of China could end up permitting happy ending massage while it is still forbidden in the land of the free. Only time will tell.

Prices for happy ending massages at parlors in the People's Republic range widely. Depending on the place rates can be the equivalent of anywhere from 10 to 100 dollars for a body rub and happy ending by hand.

Hong Kong and Macau

Nowhere in the world is happy ending massage more developed than in Hong Kong. Next door in Macau there are also many men's spas that offer massage and a whole lot more.

Now an official part of the People's Republic of China, but officially labeled as "Special Administrative Regions" with their own laws and standards, Hong Kong and Macau have maintained legal sex work. The practice is widespread across both territories.

In terms of happy ending massage there are basically two types of places in Hong Kong. First there are the run of the mill massage parlors where hand jobs happy endings are regularly provided to paying male customers. On top of that, there exists a number of high class spas with happy ending massages on their menus.

In Hong Kong there are several places where guys can check in and spend time using the facilities and getting a massage. Massages are provided by Chinese women who range in terms of looks but are mainly all skilled in the art of sensual services. Depending on the place, anything from a hand job to oral sex or even full service can be offered to customers.

Across the water in Macau things are more centered in large men's saunas that some have described as a sort of "heaven on earth" for men.

Those saunas are usually attached to large hotels or casinos. They're so open and well known that promotional packages are sold for them in the local ferry stations and four and five star hotels give men coupons for the saunas when they check in for a stay.

The men's saunas typically have a set price for entry, but

it is usually waved for customers who spend money on services inside which are sold individually.

After showering customers are free to roam the elaborate facilities which are filled with attractive women. Large swimming pools and hot tubs are staffed with women in bikinis. Shower rooms are staffed by ladies who wash customers from head to toe and sometimes throw in oral sex in between scrubbing and rinsing. Very thorough table showers are also available.

Customers can partake in these service or all sorts of elaborate massages that range from the thoroughly therapeutic to the fully erotic.

In between partaking in services customers can sit on large comfortable recliners in huge lounges filled with televisions and high speed WiFi connections. A wide range of foods is provided to customers free of charge on an unlimited basis and women are on hand to do everything from ear cleaning to foot massages for customers as they relax.

Sensual services abound and are often related to massage. A popular service is the ball or thigh massage which involves a masseuse masturbating a customer either under a towel in the public lounge or in a small private room with a reclining chair and flat screen television playing porn. The women who provide this service are skilled at doing a long erotic penis massage without bringing their customers to a climax.

When inside these saunas, customers can also view a line up of scantly clad women available for full service. If they select one of the women they head to a large and well decorated private room with a huge bed and big shower area where bathing is followed by oral and full service sex.

The women on staff come from places like mainland China, Indonesia, Vietnam, Thailand and Mongolia, with the occasional Korean or Russian also making an appearance. As a general rule the women are all good looking.

Attendants and managers also abound. They are very attentive to customers and are always available to answer any question or otherwise offer assistance.

Admission to these places allows customers to stay between 12 and 24 hours. Rooms are available for customers to sleep on premises but some prefer to simply snooze in any of the large comfortable chairs in the lounges.

Prices the services in these places range from the inexpensive to the pricey. A guy can spend a full day inside getting all sorts of erotic and non-erotic services and leave with a bill that is the equivalent of several hundred US dollars. On the other hand a guy can limit the services he partakes in and spend just a few hundred bucks.

Taiwan

Taiwan is home to a somewhat large commercial sex industry but very little of it is visible to those who don't go looking. A lot the industry is related to massage for the same reasons that sex services are commonly offered alongside massage services in many other countries around the world.

While not nearly as common as they are in Macau, men's saunas do exist in Taiwan in some numbers. Often they are hidden in plain site inside of shopping centers and the like. Inside these places, which operate much like Macau saunas with lounges, massage rooms, and dining areas, there are often discreet areas where scantly clad Chinese women deliver erotic massages that include full body rub downs, a lot of licking and full service sex with a condom.

The Taiwan saunas are nearly as open as their counterparts in Macau. Rates are a little different too. A round of full service usually goes for 4200 New Taiwan Dollars ($136 USD).

There are also some massage parlors in Taiwan that label themselves with the word "Thai." These massage parlors rarely have anything to do with either Thailand or Thai massage. Instead they are usually staffed by Chinese women who do oil massages. It's not uncommon for these women to offer hand job happy endings to male clients.

Finally there are a handful of spa style massage parlors around with the most probably being located in Taipei.

These spas tend to look like mainstream spas or beauty centers at first. However, once male customers go inside and pay a fee of around 1500 New Taiwan Dollars ($50 USD) they are led to semi-hidden sections of buildings filled with showers and private cubicles.

After showering, customers head inside those cubicles where they receive mediocre massages from scantly clad women who offer them more. Many of the women are Vietnamese with most being in their thirties.

Rates for erotic services in these spas are negotiated between providers and the clients. Some typical prices are 1000 New Taiwan Dollars ($32 USD) for a hand job and 5000 NTD ($162 USD) for full service.

Regular "mainstream" massage parlors do exist in Taiwan in some number but the people who work inside of them are unlikely to provide any erotic services.

Singapore

Singapore is widely consider to be one of the most restrictive countries in the entire world. It is perhaps counter-intuitive then that the sale of sex is legal inside the small but prosperous city state.

Legal prostitution is seemingly restricted to a number of brothels that staff women who are regularly checked for disease. Outside of such places however there is a gray market of masseuses and massage parlors that regularly offer erotic massage.

Numerous small massage parlors located in shopping centers such as Orchard Towers – a place commonly referred to as "four floors of whores" – staffed by older women are known to offer short massage with hand job happy endings for around 100 Singapore Dollars ($72 USD).

There are also all sorts of massage parlors and masseuses around Singapore who offer massage followed by a hand job or more. All sorts of names are applied for this sort of service, but the women who provide it are usually referred to as massage girls or massage technicians.

Finally there are the "health centers." These places operate somewhat like the aforementioned men's saunas in other countries with a large Chinese presence.

There are at least one hundred of these so-called health centers in Singapore. Sexual services are offered in many, if not most of them.

The facilities in these health centers are rarely great. Most people would probably not even describe many of them as good. Customers can either pay a fee to use the sauna facilities or opt to go straight to a private room for a massage. With either option they are soon introduced to service providers inside.

The service providers can range in looks but most would probably be considered attractive by nearly all men. They typically provide a few minutes of mediocre massage followed by offers for more. Rates can vary and are subject to negotiation but some general prices seem to have established in these sorts of places. Hand jobs usually go for around 40 Singapore Dollars ($29 USD), blow jobs usually go for closer to 75 SGD ($55 USD), and full service goes for 100 SGD ($73 YSD) and up.

Some of the street walkers who offer sexual services to customers in parts of Singapore like Geylang sometimes couch their services in massage terms too.

Malaysia

Malaysia is one of the larger Muslim majority countries in the world. All sorts of rules are in place that many from developed countries would probably consider restrictive to say the least. Still, there are many erotic massage providers in the country.

Kuala Lumpur is without a doubt home to the most erotic massage parlors in the country. They operate in various levels of openness. Some are more hidden than others.

The various men's spas in Kuala Lumpur operate a lot like the previously described health centers in Singapore or oily massage parlors in Thailand. Customers enter and are shown a lineup of the available service providers who tend to be attractive. The ladies are variously Chinese, Vietnamese, Thai, Uzbek, Indonesian or even Malay.

Sessions in these spas typically involve little to no actual massage. Instead customers are showered then given a blow job followed by full service sex. Prices for standard services range between 230 and 300 Ringgit ($56-74 USD).

On top of the more sexually oriented spas there are also countless mainstream and Thai massage parlors around.

Many of the Thai massage parlors have black tinted glass and lock their doors in between customers. Many of the same places also offer hand jobs for 50 Ringgit ($12 USD) on top of the regular massage price of 60 Ringgit ($15 USD) per hour.

Some of the regular massage parlors which resemble the standard massage parlors in a city like Bangkok also staff women who offer extras. Anything from a hand job to full service can be offered to customers by these ladies, though obviously not every masseuse makes such services available.

The largest concentration of massage parlors in all of Malaysia is undoubtedly located along Changkat Bukit Bintang. There numerous women from all around Asia call out to people who pass by offering massage. Some of them offer sensual services in private.

Indonesia

Indonesia is the widely described as "the largest Muslim country in the world." I'll leave aside the question of whether or not a country can have a religion and get right down to the point. Despite widespread conservationism rooted in religion that emerges often in the country, Indonesia is actually home to a truly massive commercial sex scene.

There are many massage parlors in Indonesia that cater to men. They operate much like the male spas in Kuala Lumpur. Guys enter, pay a fee, and get a short massage followed by an erotic massage of one kind or another given by a woman on staff. Some places like Kartika even offer soapy body slides like soapies in Thailand. Prices of 350,000 Rupiah ($24 USD) are fairly common.

One of the most famous massage parlors for foreigners was Maribaya Massage on the sixth floor of Jakarta's Hotel Melawai I. It was basically a brothel where full service sex was offered for 400,000 Rupiah ($28 USD). It is now closed, but others like it remain.

Beyond the regular massage places and massage front brothels, there are also several very large entertainment complexes in Indonesia. Many like the famous Alexis Hotel are located in Jakarta.

These places operate a lot like the Macau men's saunas but with a less closed atmosphere. They often have multiple floors that can include everything from a disco dance club to a strip club or massage parlor. Regular massages are often offered on the cheap while a bevy of women from various areas offer "massage" that is really bathing and full service for anywhere from 325,000 to 1,000,000 Rupiah ($22-69 USD). These places mainly cater to locals and Asian businessmen but they don't seem to turn foreigners away.

Recently, moves have been made against some rather large establishments reported to offer sexual services, often under the guise of massage. Some smaller places have been closed too. There seems to be a real clamoring against sex work of all kinds, even in Jakarta.

In the future erotic massage may disappear all together from Indonesia, or more likely be driven into the dark depths of the underground. On the other hand, there may be some sort of reversal that allows the large local scene to blossom into something even bigger. Only time will tell.

Colombia

Prostitution is legal and widespread in Colombia. Most commonly sex is sold out of brothels, strip clubs, apartments, and on the street. Happy ending massage does exist however, especially in the mountain town of Medellin.

Erotic massage parlors in Medellin are somewhat discreet and hidden from plain view but they are not necessarily underground. They exist in main parts of the city and usually advertise online.

Massage parlors like the well known Jade Palace Spa are set up more or less like standard massage parlors except that they are often located because discreet private doors and above street level.

Inside these kinds of places have lobbies with front desk staffs or managers where payment is rendered. For a fee start at around 150,000 Pesos ($50 USD) customers get a one hour session that normally starts with a short bit of mediocre massage followed by a quick transition into full service.

The women who work at these sorts of massage parlors are normally in their twenties or maybe thirties. Most men would probably find them all to be at least somewhat attractive.

The Dominican Republic

The Dominican Republic has a famously large commercial sex industry but very little of it is in any way involved with massage.

A German owned place called Passions in the seaside town of Sosua grew from a small massage parlor offering full service sex to a large complex complete with a go go bar stage and private rooms. It was eventually shuttered by the authorities however after it was claimed the place broke laws regarding the sale of sex in the country.

There are still some small massage parlors in Sosua staffed mostly by Haitian women who do happy ending massages on the cheap, but even some of those have been shut down by authorities who claim to be on a mission to "clean up the city."

Germany and Austria

Prostitution is legal in both Germany and Austria. The sale of sex goes on in all sorts of above ground legal venues. In some cases sexual services are also offered in a more gray area through places listed as massage shops.

Massage shops offering happy ending are not necessarily common in either country, but they are not rare either.

In both Austria and Germany there are some places posing as massage parlors that are basically brothels in reality. They tend to staff Chinese women even when they have shop names that reference Japan. Typical prices start at around 50 Euros for a short session. Some of these places such as Asia Studio Wien in Vienna advertise openly while others are more discreet.

Many of the massage shops listed as Thai massage parlors in Germany offer hand job happy endings to male customers often with no tipping required. These places are staffed by Thai women and offer real Thai massages for prices of around 60 Euros ($68 USD). This stands in stark contrast to South Korea where as I explained earlier Thai massage parlors usually do not offer erotic massage of any kind.

Prostate Massage

A final note is probably deserved for something that has become a bit of a trend in the world of erotic massage over the last few years: the prostate massage.

The prostate is a gland involved with the male reproductive system normally accessed through the rectum. Now that the biology lesson is over, let's move on to the rest of the information.

Prostate massage can be done with fingers or other objects inserted into the anus. For some time, it was almost solely performed by physicians attempting to treat chronic prostatitis. They massaged the prostate either by hand or with the aid of things like a heated metal rod. After studies showed that this was no more effective than the use of antibiotic medicine alone, the practice was discontinued. Some physicians may now be providing similar treatment, but as far as I know it no longer has widespread acceptance in the medical community. Of course, I am no medical expert.

I have not experienced such treatment, but I can't imagine it is much different than a digital rectal exam which is uncomfortable but recommended for men of a certain age by most doctors.

Why all this medical talk? As far as I know, prostate massage has it roots in such treatment. Sure others play around with the anus for fun during sex, but "prostate massage" as a set sort of thing seems to have been established by doctors. Coincidentally, the same is said about vibrators for women which were originally sold to treat "hysteria," but that's another subject.

There are now masseuses all around the world who offer

prostate massage on request or even as a standard service. Apparently it is now quite popular.

Earlier it was rarely mentioned. Customers either requested it from trusted erotic massage providers in private or the providers themselves suggested it when their hands were already in the area. In same cases things still go that way. In others, such as in the many "kinky massage parlors" located on Bangkok's Sukhumvit Soi 22, prostate massage is openly listed on menus.

In some places like the US or Japan where prostate massage might be viewed as a premium service, it can come with a high price tag. At other places like Akane Massage in Bangkok, it is included with a regular erotic massage session that costs as little as $36 US.

While some men swear by prostate massage as method to achieve mind-blowing climax, others want nothing to do with it.

As it turns out, there are plenty of risks associated with the practice. Even medical professionals can cause fissures, septicemia, and the spread of prostatitis when performing a prostate massage. One can only imagine the damage a person with no medical training could cause.

Still, plenty of men get prostate massages on a regular basis with no complications and the practice only seems to be getting more common with each passing day.

Ultimately, life is a series of risks. A prostate massage may be risky. So may an erotic massage in an underground establish. Then again crossing the street can be risky too. Not every chicken gets to the other side.

Disclaimer

The author does not advocate any illegal activities. In fact, he does not advocate anything at all. This book was written purely for educational and entertainment purposes. The reader assumes all risks and responsibilities for their own actions.

The facts are the facts. Those who can't deal with them might best be served by a cold shower or perhaps even some counseling.

As they say: your mileage may vary.

Also available from the Author:

Paying for Sex: A Global Guide to Prostitution

Blowjob Bars: The Complete Report

Prostitution in Berlin: The Complete Report

Prostitution in Taipei: The Complete Report

Prostitution in Frankfurt: The Complete Report

Prostitution in Vienna: The Complete Report

Prostitution in Macau: The Complete Report

Prostitution in Jakarta: The Complete Report

Sex Talk : Discussions with Prostitutes, Porn Stars, Producers, Photographers and Penmen

www.RockitReports.com